Personal Religion

PERSONAL
RELIGION

By Herbert C. Alleman

Muhlenberg Press : Philadelphia

1947

248
AL5p

23790
nov 47

To my Brother and my Sister

Contents

		Page
1.	PERSONAL RELIGION	1
2.	SOLILOQUY	7
3.	GOD	11
4.	IN TWO WORLDS	15
5.	THE BETTER PART	19
6.	THE DRAG OF OUR HUMAN NATURE	23
7.	A WAY OF LIFE	29
8.	FAITH	33
9.	SPEECH AND SILENCE	39
10.	PRAYER	45
11.	CONDUCT, THE BADGE OF PERSONAL RELIGION	51
12.	A GOOD CONSCIENCE	55
13.	STEWARDSHIP	59
14.	CONVICTION	65
15.	STRENGTHENING THE WILL	71
16.	GOOD CHEER	75
17.	TEMPTATION	81
18.	CHARACTER	87
19.	THE CHURCH	93
20.	OUR LEADER	97
21.	THE BIBLE	103
22.	THE SACRAMENTS	109
23.	"WHAT THINK YE OF CHRIST?"	115
24.	ETERNAL LIFE	121

A man's religion is the chief fact with regard to him.

Thomas Carlyle

1
Personal Religion

"A MAN's religion," says Thomas Carlyle, "is the chief fact with regard to him." But he hastens to add, "By religion I do not mean the church creed which he professes, the articles of faith which he will sign and, in words or otherwise, assert. . . . This is not what I call religion . . . but the thing a man does practically lay to heart, and know for certain, concerning his vital relation to the mysterious universe, and his duty and destiny there." [1]

That religion we call *personal religion*. It is at once evident that it means the religion of the individual as over against the religion of the group. It is interesting to note that "personal" comes from the Latin word *persona*, meaning a mask covering the whole head, which ancient players wore and changed according to the character to be represented. The "person" was the character represented by the actor. A person, therefore, was a distinct individual, originally an individual of note, a personage. Then the word came to be the designation of any human being — man or woman or child — a self-conscious, self-determining individual as indicated by his distinctive and individual traits. Later it came to stand for the human form in its characteristic completeness, the body of the living man, woman, or child, the external appearance which singles one out by its distinctive marks.

---

[1] *Heroes and Hero Worship*, Lecture I.

"Personal," therefore, is that which belongs to one-self.

"Religion" is the communion between the worshiping person and the worshiped object, the communion of a man with what he conceives to be his maker or the power that controls his destiny. It involves recognition of and allegiance to that power by word and life. The God of the Christian being a moral Person, the expression of the Christian religion in life is in accordance with the character of the deity. The character of the deity determines the character of the religion.

Personal religion is religion at the fountain source in the soul. In this age of collectivism we have been so engrossed with corporate expression that we have lost a sharp sense of personal responsibility. There is much need for the recovery of personal religion. It is shown by the most cursory survey of the moral and cultural standards of our day. The loss of the practice of personal religion is symbolized, says Professor George F. Thomas, by the disuse of the word "saint" in the New Testament sense, and in such expressions as "the communion of saints." Its disappearance has been attended by a weakening of the spiritual life in all its phases. The midweek prayer meeting in the Protestant churches, called by our fathers "the pulse of the church," has given way to the "social hour." "The dominant ideal of character in recent generations," says Prof. Thomas, "has been that of the congenial, sociable, adjusted person who pleases everyone but lacks moral principle and spiritual depth." [2] Personal religion has

---

[2] *The Christian Answer*, Charles Scribner's Sons, 1945.

simply not been an objective in his life. In a similar way the loss of the passion for personal perfection has shown itself in the shallowness of our culture. It is not that our generation is without intensity. Our application to the mastery of technology has wrought wonders. We have multiplied the production of all manner of creature comforts. We have lifted the burden from the bent back of labor. We have prolonged the span of human life. We have redeemed the wastelands of continents. We have made the state function as a nursing father. But life — personal life — has been left to chance, to grow wild, to exist without succor from the realm of the spirit.

It has been said that a man reveals his essential religion by what he does with his leisure. In other words, the depth of his soul is shown by the pleasures he indulges in. If that is so, what are we to say of the personal religion of most of us? Technology has been busy here. It has not only lengthened the hours of our leisure, but it has given us a system of mass exploitation of our spare time. By the use of the new technique in providing commercialized entertainment for the masses, industrial science has capitalized on what it has discovered as the line of least resistance. The captains of technological amusements say they give the people what they want. What an indictment of our souls is the "movie," the radio, the play, the dance, the comic strip of our day! "Few of us realize," said Dr. C. C. Morrison in *The Christian Century*, "how drenched our minds are with the flood of nonsense and silliness and grotesquerie and artificiality and vulgarity and profanity with which clever technicians intrigue our attention." Do we really like that sort of thing? Do we want to associate with the kind of people whom we watch disporting their inanities before us? Does our presence in their company reflect our own inner life? If it does, is it not high time for us to enter into the secret place of the soul, to commune with our hearts, to ask ourselves what we are doing with our lives and what is our essential religion?

In our crowded world we are lonely because we are never alone.

O. P. Kretzmann

2
Soliloquy

SOLILOQUY is the mother tongue of religion. "Solitude is the audience-chamber of God." We are not surprised, therefore, to find a great deal of soliloquy in the Bible. How many of the Psalms are talks with one's own soul! "I communed with mine own heart and my spirit made diligent search." As we read the Psalms how often we forget that it is not ourselves who are speaking, testing our own hearts with questions, reasoning ourselves out of the gloom of despondency into the joy of confidence!

The Book of Ecclesiastes is an annotated soliloquy. *Qoheleth*, the title of the book, is a feminine participle. It was probably the diary of a primitive teacher of philosophy. The experiments recounted were all in the writer's own mind. We have the clue in the words which preface each in turn: "I communed with mine own heart, saying. . . ."

Soliloquy characterizes the parables of our Lord. There is the rich husbandman in the midst of crops too bountiful for him to store — the disclosure of what he worshiped — who talked with his soul thus: "Soul, thou hast much goods laid up for many years; take thine ease, eat, drink, and be merry." It is not necessary for the parable to declare his folly. Already we have said, "Thou fool." On the other hand, the Prodigal Son comes to himself in soliloquy: "How many hired servants of my father's have bread enough and to spare, and I perish with

hunger. I will arise and go to my father, and will say
unto him, Father, I have sinned against heaven and before
thee, and am no more worthy to be called thy son: make
me as one of thy hired servants."

The gist of philosophy (wisdom), said Socrates, is
"Know thyself." It is the key to the solution of the
riddle of life. The Oriental objectified his soul and con-
versed with it as his *alter ego*. This helped him to understand the life that was going on within him. It enabled
him to get his bearings, to see how many of the things he
was doing were worth while. Out of that practice came
the "school" and the "college" and the "seminary,"
originally groups of kindred minds, separated from the
distractions of mundane life, to contemplate the things of
the soul under the guidance of trusted teachers. They
were places of retreat from the busy life and distractions
of the world. In the older colleges for women, such as
Wellesley and Smith, "the quiet hour" was observed. At
the beginning and at the close of the day there was a brief
period when every student was in her room. The halls
were silent. There was no prescribed way of spending
these periods. They were invitations to introspection,
that the students might learn to know themselves.

One of the great needs of our day is a silent time amid
the noise and bustle of modern life, an hour when the busy
activities of all other hours shall cease, when we shall with-
draw our souls into the inner court of self-communion.
"In our crowded world," says Dr. O. P. Kretzmann, "we
are lonely because we are never alone. . . . No time to go
to where prayer is the only sound and God the only

light." [1] Time was when a part of the life of the Christian home was the retirement of all the members of the family to their own rooms for a brief season of self-communion. Our modern homes do not have many rooms. We are so much away from home that the small lad's answer to his Sunday-school teacher's question, "What is your home?" fairly reflects our modern life, "My home is the place where we keep the things we buy." The garage and the home — of almost equal size — are of almost equal importance. Activism has well-nigh banished meditation. As a consequence our spiritual life, broadly speaking, is shallow. An almost grotesque spectacle is witnessed in our spasmodic efforts to regain spirituality by cavalcades and retreats to somewhere else than where we live. One good purpose they serve; they remind us that we are pilgrims and strangers here.

Neither activism nor legerdemain can take the place of honest self-examination. Get the habit of communing with your own heart. Question your soul about the things you are doing. Ask yourself, am I deceiving myself in my life? What sort of person am I? Do I care more for appearance than for reality? Am I spending my days in the pursuit of the things which perish in the using? Am I laying up treasure that shall not be taken away from me in the hour of death? Then ask yourself one question more, Soul, what thinkest thou of Christ — apart from the books and the doctors, apart from the world and the fashion of it — soul, what thinkest thou of Christ?

---

[1] *The Pilgrim*, Concordia Publishing House, St. Louis.

God is our refuge and strength, a very present help in trouble.

Psalm 46

3
God

RELIGION is the first preoccupation of personality. We are fundamentally religious. We have a background, and that background is God. Men instinctively believe there is a God, and that we stand in relation to Him. Men may train their minds to atheism, but atheism is never instinctive. It is the testimony of history that men are by nature aware of a Power with which they have to do and which primarily thwarts them. The Power must be appeased or bribed. Because conscience has survived the appalling catastrophe which we call the Fall, the Power is looked upon by aboriginal man as hostile.

Religion does not become personal until we know God as personal. As long as men knew deity only as Power that thwarted them, they could not think of Him as a being who was friendly. The nature-religions did not look upon the universe as friendly. The religion of India included the worship of Siva, the destroyer. There must be something in the world which seeks to mar all good order, so Siva the destroyer was set up alongside Vishnu, the creator. Thus the gods multiplied. Men made new gods for each phase of their needs. The higher the intelligence of man in the ancient world, the greater the number of the gods. Egypt numbered them in hundreds, Babylonia in thousands. The result was that the dominant note of all ancient nature-religions was fear. No one could be sure that the Power was satisfied. The mind of man did not evolve monotheism. It is a matter of revelation, of which the Bible is the record.

Inspiration will always remain something of a mystery. Why the idea of one God, and He not hostile but friendly, whose purposes are benevolent, should have come to the fathers of the Hebrew people and not to the nations around them of higher culture and more advanced civilization, has no more reasonable answer than that the attitude of their thinkers and teachers opened the door to its reception. Their faith did not spring into existence full-fledged like Apollo from the head of Zeus. There was still much that baffled them, still much in their lives which could breed only heavy thoughts and haunting fears; but let a man seek refuge in God alone and learn to know Him as He was revealing Himself in history, hearken unto His voice and seek to keep in right relation with Him, and he could go on and endure and overcome. The God whom the Hebrew teachers revealed is a personal God, a God not far off but nigh at hand, a God to whom we can speak and who speaks to us.

That is what makes the God of the Bible different from all the gods of the nations. Our God speaks, and He is the only God who does. We have His Word, which means that we may have fellowship with Him, and personal religion is that fellowship. If one would learn how to speak to Him, let him turn to the Book of Psalms, the outpouring of the individual believer, "the forgotten man" in a totalitarian world. The psalmists' nation perished, the people went into exile. They lost their land, but they did not lose their God.

Out of such experience came Psalm 46. It was never more indicated as a rallying hymn than now. If the world which confronted the original singer was one of desolation, what would its author say of ours? Institutions which we called mountains of strength have almost literally been carried into the midst of the sea. What hope is there for a world like this? The answer is *God*. "Be still and know that I am God." He has turned haughty world powers to desolation. He has brought deliverance and peace to the lands that have honored Him. Let His people contemplate this and relax the tension and strain of fear. There is one supreme and controlling Power in the world — it is God. He is our Rock and our Salvation, our Refuge and Strength.

But the Christian has something more. We have the Word made flesh. We have Jesus Christ and His own religion. He brought religion out of the realm of the abstract into the concrete. The key to Jesus' religion is the way He thought of God. God was the Father. That definitely makes religion personal. If God is our Father, then heaven presents a kindly face to our weaknesses. A Father does not give up a wayward child. "Your heavenly Father also forgiveth you." Similarly all the relations and duties of life are under the Father. Our relation to the Father makes obligation. The will of the Father creates our duties. The revelation of the Father dispels our doubts. The comfort of the Father illumines our toils and trials. The relation of the Father determines our relation to one another. How little we remember that we are the children of the Father!

How shall we sing the Lord's song in a strange land?

Psalm 137

4
In Two Worlds

PSALM 137 is an ancient folk song which lends itself to a modern setting. One would like to substitute it for some of the maudlin ditties included in contemporary radio programs. It would be incongruous, but it would "point a moral."

There is no clue to the date of the Psalm; that is the art of it. We think only of the psalmist's emotions. They oscillate between Jerusalem and Babylon. Now he is in exile in Babylon; the heartbreak of his situation throbs in every line of the Psalm. The Euphrates made Babylon, and its shores and canal banks, like water fronts everywhere, were the resort of men in every mood. The Hebrew exiles "sat," the posture of mourning (Job 2:8), and, after a vain attempt to sing the songs of Zion, they hung their harps on the willows. They could not sing the songs of Zion there. Their Babylonian neighbors, touched by the deep devotion of the singers, asked them to continue: "Sing to us some of those songs of Zion," thinking they were only characteristic folk songs. These plunderers, whose armies had despoiled and wasted their beloved country, would turn their hymns into ditties! It could not be done. The songs of Zion could not be sung for the idle entertainment of Gentiles in a foreign land.

Which things are an allegory. Babylon stands for "the world" of the New Testament, that which constitutes the sum of things as organized apart from God, the visible and transitory order of human life and its interests as over against the invisible and eternal. It is described in the New Testament as stemming from the lust of the flesh and the lust of the eyes and the pride of life. Its essence is attachment to the things which seem "good for food, and a delight to the eyes," "the proud display of life," the pleasures, the pursuits, and the rewards of the present world — the world that "knows us not," says St. John, "because it knew him (our Lord) not." There is no common denominator between them.

The difference between the Christian and the man of the world is not always apparent, but it is real. It is like the International Rift in the Thousand Islands, whose walls at times come so close that the branches of the trees almost overarch the channel and screen the water. From the sky the land might seem to be one island, but on one side is the Dominion of Canada while on the other floats the Stars and Stripes. The boatmen of both shores ply their trade among all the islands of the river, but they carry different licenses and own different allegiances.

There may be superficial companionships between the men of these two worlds, but sooner or later the issue is drawn and we must take our stand and assert our allegiance. The answer is not asceticism. Jesus Christ came eating and drinking. Monasticism was born of a different spirit. What Jesus did for us was to create a priority in our affections for the things of the Spirit. Every man has a ruling passion. Sooner or later every man will reveal the "commonwealth" to which he belongs. The challenge came to the Hebrew exiles when the Babylonian idlers asked them to sing some of the songs of Zion for their entertainment. It may come to us in the common pleasure hall or the narrow circle of congenial associates. Many years ago Sir Robert Peel was a guest at a dinner given by one of his political associates. When the conversation turned on religion, and stories were told of the hypocrisy of church people, and the sentiment was expressed that the Christian religion was a sham, Sir Robert arose and asked his host to call his carriage, remarking, "I am still a Christian, gentlemen."

Jesus is continually standing over against "the lust of the flesh." "Will ye also go away?" He asked of the Twelve as His eyes followed "the many" who, having eaten of the loaves and the fishes, went back and no longer walked with Him. "Bread from heaven" did not interest them. Louder than any protests of their lips their act told to which world they belonged. We are glad for those brave words of Peter: "Lord, to whom shall we go? You have the words of eternal life." The line was drawn. That side lay the old, easy life with the loaves and fishes of sensuous satisfaction; this side lies the flinty path to the cross and eternal life. The two worlds are poised before us. To which do we belong?

We proudly bear as banner
A cross within the heart,
To show that we have chosen
Christ, the better part.

Lillian Weaver Cassaday

5
The Better Part

The New York Times of June 3, 1944, announced under a bold-face caption that on the following day Dr. George William Edwards would be ordained to the priesthood of the Protestant Episcopal Church in the Cathedral of St. John the Divine. Probably the average reader did not notice it. There is nothing remarkable in the ordination of a minister. And yet this announcement made top-column, headline publicity. The explanation lies in who Dr. Edwards was. He was an economist of international reputation, a graduate of City College and Columbia University, a research agent in foreign banking for the Federal Reserve Board in the United States and in Europe, a professor of banking in New York University, an instructor on investments in the Graduate School of Banking of the American Bankers Association, the author of a half-dozen volumes on the science of banking, and then a graduate of Union Theological Seminary and of the General Seminary of the Episcopal Church. When asked why this change in his life, he replied, "The present world problems need religion more than economics — I think I have chosen the better part."

Dr. Edwards therefore qualifies as an expert witness. He knows the economic world from the inside, human life organized on the principle of secularism. Its realities are the visible, tangible things which satisfy the senses. Dr. Edwards made his decision at the apex of secularism, in "the Augustan age" of this modern world, as Dr. Richard Niebuhr has called it. He had seen the triumphs of technology: distance abolished and the resources of the world at our hand in hours; inches added to our stature and years to the span of our life; conversation around the world, with vision added to speech; the multiplication of wealth until pounds have become as insignificant as pence and only billions satisfy our sense of a sizable debt. The year of jubilee for economic man has come.

But in the hour when men envisaged Utopia and the golden age of economic security seemed about to dawn, a shadow fell across their path, reminding them that, though they gain the whole world, earth is not enough. Recently we have been impressed by an English interpretation of an old picture, "The Shadow of the Saint." After a gay revel two young girls are returning to their homes, jauntily swinging their richly dressed bodies. They are flushed with pleasure, and they are beautiful in their excitement. Life for them is at its zenith. Suddenly, on the moonlit walk, a shadow falls across their path. It is the shadow of a gaunt, weird figure kneeling on the top of a pillar, with hands uplifted in prayer. It is the shadow of Saint Simeon the pillar saint, who, according to the superstitions of the fifth century, lived for years on the narrow summit of a column. Into the hearts of those two giddy girls is suddenly flashed the contrast between the saint's life and theirs. They are living only for the things of the world; he, however crudely, is living for the things which are unseen and eternal. They do not fully understand the contrast between his life and theirs, but they are arrested by the vision of another world, a higher world than theirs, a world which opens into heaven.

That is all the picture was meant to convey, but it teaches that this world in which we are so madly immersed is neither self-sufficient nor sufficient for us. It is not self-sufficient because, with all its glamor and achievement, as one has said, "It is founded on principles which man has learned from sources which are given him in this time-sense world, namely, the unity of the universe and the intelligence and consistency of natural laws, which are preconceptions and not consequences of the world." All the programs of political and economic science rest on the conviction of the worth and dignity of man. The much-vaunted bills of human rights have validity only for those who have been living in an ideal world in which those truths are evident.

Nor is the world sufficient for us. There never was so much wealth in the world and so wide a distribution of it, never so many creature comforts, never so much leisure protected by law, never such a mastery of human ills and economic dislocations — and there never was so much chaos in human life, individual and social, as now. If internal evidence were a safe guide to authorship, the Book of Ecclesiastes was written yesterday. "The eye is not satisfied with seeing, nor the ear with hearing . . . neither is his eye satisfied with riches. . . . He that loveth silver shall not be satisfied with silver, nor he that loveth abundance with increase. . . ." These are the confessions of our world as well as of his. The shadow of the higher world is upon us. Dr. Edwards saw it and chose the better part.

For all the nations of the world seek these things; and your Father knows that you need them. Instead, seek his kingdom, and these things shall be yours as well.

Luke 12:30, 31
(from the Revised Standard Version of the New Testament)

6
The Drag of Our Human Nature

HAVING chosen the better part, why should the way be hard? Why must we be hedged about with restrictions? Why do not men live together as children of a common Father? Why must we have gates and guards, jails and penalties, in order to secure a modicum of social order? When we press the question why this is so, we are carried back to the beginning of human history. The Bible begins with that question. Man was made in the likeness of God. He was the highest work of God's creation. He was given mind and language, which made fellowship with God possible. Why was that fellowship ever broken? God did not break it. Why did not man continue to live in this fellowship?

The answer to our question is found in one word — our human nature. We are related to the flesh as well as to the Spirit, and the things of the flesh catch our eye more quickly than the things of the Spirit. We allow our appetites, our lower desires, to cheat us of what is good for us. That is what the Bible tells us happened with the first man. We were appalled at the devastation wrought by the atomic bomb, and still shrink with shame and horror at the obliteration of Nagasaki and Hiroshima. But what was that compared with the ruin to human life when man released his God-given freedom in the pursuit of sensuous satisfactions and brought upon him the bondage of the flesh? Genesis 3 is moral history. It is the history of *our* Fall — not Adam's, as a solitary person. Adam is man. How vivid the tragedy becomes in a modern setting! Robert Louis Stevenson's *The Strange Case of Dr. Jekyll and Mr. Hyde* is a classic because it is a timeless rescript of human experience. The confession of Dr. Jekyll is Romans 7 spoken by a contemporary.

But we are not like that, the slaves of our appetites. There are Dr. Jekylls, but, thank God, they are the exceptions. Most of us are not criminals; we are merely worldlings. In one of his charming books Anatole France pictures himself in a throng of gay Neapolitans crowding about a much-patronized tavern. "They live," he says, "through all their senses at the same time; and, being philosophers without knowing it, keep the measure of their desires in accordance with the brevity of life." Above the entrance is a quatrain which, being translated, reads: "Friends, let us merrily eat and drink as long as oil remains in the lamp. Who knows whether we shall meet again in the other world? Who knows whether in the other world there be a tavern?" "Ever thus," muses the poet-author, "the sight of a fair land under a spotless sky urges to the pursuit of quiet pleasures." "But," he concludes, "there are souls forever harassed by some sublime discontent; they are the noblest . . . in the age of Christianity, the souls of the saints, and the 'Golden Legend' is full of the miracles they wrought." [1]

"Take no thought," says Jesus, "for what ye shall eat, or what ye shall drink, or wherewithal ye shall be clothed.

---

[1] *The Crime of Sylvestre Bonnard*, Harper & Brothers, New York.

. . . After all these things do the Gentiles seek. But seek ye first the kingdom of God." He is saying that to us, the common run of people with our schedule of sensuous pleasures far overbalancing our schedule of religion. We see far more of our friends in the social hall, at the club, at the card table, in the "tavern," than we do in church and church school and community aid centers. A pastor had just preached a sermon on Heaven when one of his "society" faithful came to him and said: "Do you know, my idea of heaven is just G——— with the disagreeable people left out." Yes, he knew. "Who knows whether in the other world there be a tavern?"

That is the story of our human nature. The problem of personal religion is to recover the spiritual power that has been lost. Christians find that power in Christ. He gave us the power by showing us the way back to God, removing our misconceptions of religion, taking away our fear of God, mediating His forgiving love, sharing His Spirit with us — in a word, making new men of us. To get that power we must retrace the steps by which we lost it. In his farewell to the Ephesian elders Paul gave us the formula of recovery: "Repentance toward God and faith toward our Lord Jesus Christ" (Acts 20:21). Repentance means not only the recognition of our mistake and sorrow for it, but the taking of Christ's way of life instead of our own. That will bring us back to a right relation to God and to life lived as in His world. The supreme act of personal religion is to accept what Christ offers to all men and to each individually.

God never meant to let our poor weak human nature

defeat the purposes of His love. In Jesus Christ He has made Himself one with us, taking a human personality that He might suffer and share with us, becoming our partner in the reconstruction of our lives. There is no plane of human experience upon which God in Jesus Christ has not stood by man's side. He has made it possible for us to overcome the drag of our human nature. This He will do if we accept what He offers; but the act of acceptance is ours. It is the most important act of personal religion.

Teacher, we know that you are true, and care for no man; for you do not regard the position of men, but truly teach the way of God.

Mark 12:14
(from the Revised Standard Version of the New Testament)

7
A Way of Life

THE Christian religion in its personal exercise is a way of life. As such it is not self-originated. The Christian Church is the fellowship of the "called." The New Testament word for "church" (*ecclesia*) means just that. In the Old Testament Israel was "the called" of God. "Now Jehovah said unto Abram, Get thee out of thy country and from thy kindred" (Gen. 12:1). Moses was called to lead his people out of Egypt (Ex. 3:10ff). But they were not merely called and left to their own devices. Each was called into a covenant with its peculiar marks. The former had the badge of circumcision, which stood for a distinctive way of life. The latter had the badge of conduct, which was specified in the Decalogue. The ten "words," as the Bible calls them, were not prohibitions in the sense in which we use the term. They are specifications of the things which, in the covenant relation, are not done. They describe the way of life lived by those who responded to the call of their God. Their observance constituted the human side of the covenant relation. As the Hebrew indicates, these "commandments" should be translated, not "Thou shalt not," but "Thou wilt not." It was not until the "words" of Sinai came into competition with the laws of surrounding nations that there came to be codes of Israel known as the Law. As her laws multiplied and her life was more and more hedged in by restrictions, Israel's greatness declined. Precepts multiplied, freedom departed. Keeping the Law became an end in itself; it was no longer a way of life inspired by the character of its God. It was blind legalism inspired by fear.

We are people of the New Covenant. The Christian religion began with Jesus Christ. He was not merely one more rabbi with new laws to add to the multitude of precepts that were weighing down the life of His people. He came to deliver men from the thraldom of the meticulous. He taught us the way to live the good life by being so filled with the Spirit that there was no room for the bad life. He would have us not only lop off the fruits of the bad life, but uproot it. He condemned not only the act but the thought that produced the act. We are not only not to commit murder, we are not to hate. We are not only not to commit adultery, we are not to harbor lascivious thoughts out of which adultery flowers. We are not only not to take false oaths, we are to beware of untruthfulness which seems to make oaths necessary. "Let your speech be, Yea, yea; Nay, nay: for whatsoever is more than these cometh of evil." Laws are made for people in the mass; obedience is a matter of the individual conscience.

In his *Autobiography* G. K. Chesterton says that when arranging for a room with a landlady the first question that should be asked is not "What are your terms?" but "What is your view of the universe?" If that was right, he could trust the others. Jesus led men to the good life by awakening in them a sense of their relation to God. We talk a great deal about human relations. Jesus was always talking about our relation to God. If that was right, He could trust the others.

Life is good only in so far as God is in it. Personal religion as Jesus saw and lived it is not the keeping of a series of precepts and a program of activities; it is finding God's will in all our relations and making that will the rule of our living. That is the way Jesus lived. He was born with a human body, and He made it the temple of the Holy Spirit. He was a child of the home, and He was obedient to its necessary obligations. He grew up under the protection of the state, and He said "Render unto Caesar the things that are Caesar's." He did not rebel against its restrictions, or count their observance slavery. In a normal world there would be no restrictions, but ours is not a normal world. It remains for us to find the Christian way of life. Unless duty be lighted up with the glow of personal relationship, it will remain a thing to be escaped — such is the drag of our human nature; but with the sense of relationship with God in Jesus Christ we may sing with the psalmist, "Thy statutes have been my songs in the house of my pilgrimage."

Faith is not the holding of correct doctrine, but personal fellowship with the living God.

William Temple

FAITH lies at the very heart of personal religion. It may be said to be the key to all religion. Faith (*fides*) begins where knowledge (*scientia*) ends. "Now we know in part," and that is all we can know within the horizon of our present limitations. We are limited in our capacity to know, and we are limited by what Dr. Reinhold Niebuhr calls "the penumbra of mystery which surrounds us." There is the mystery of God, and the mystery of life, and the mystery of evil, and the mystery of death. How vast is our yearning, how small is our knowledge! So little do we know, it is the line of least resistance to say that we do not know at all.

But that has never satisfied the serious mind. God never meant that we were to be baffled by our limitations. Our souls cry out for help from above. Faith is the hand that lays hold of the Rock that is higher than we. Faith is at once the confession of our weakness and need, and the acceptance of the proffered help. Faith must have an object; we do not have faith in a vacuum. Christ is the object of Christian faith.

When we have a consensus of faith we have a creed. Creed is the expression of our common faith, which we call a confession. A mere confession, however, is not faith. Faith builds its life on what the mind accepts as true and our experience has verified. Christian faith centers in Christ, not in an institution, or a creed, or even the Bible as an end in itself. "Faith," said the late Archbishop Temple, "is not the holding of correct doctrine, but personal fellowship with the living God. . . . I do not believe in any creed, but I use certain creeds to express, to conserve, and to deepen my belief in God. What is offered to man's apprehension in any specific revelation is not truth concerning God, but the living God Himself." [1] It is a popular thought today that in Jesus Christ we have a new *conception* of God. That is true, but it is not the conception of God which is the object of our faith. Faith is not the acceptance of that conception with the mind. It is something deeper; it is the laying hold of the source of that conception with our surrendered will and giving Him our allegiance.

Jesus Christ does not ask to be patronized; He asks to be followed. And He is to be followed in this very matter of faith. A Christian ought to trust in God as Jesus trusted in Him. The key to Jesus' trust in God is the way He thought of Him. God is the Father, His Father and all men's Father. He said to the men and women who thronged about Him, Think of God as Father and you will understand God; and think of yourselves as children of the Father and you will understand yourselves. That will solve our questions as to whether we can know God, whether we can confidently pray to Him, whether we can face the future with hope. A world created by the Father did not come into being by accident. A world governed by the Father is not left to chance. He who

---

[1] *Nature, Man and God,* The Macmillan Company, New York, 1935.

clothes the flowers and feeds the birds will not be un-
mindful of His children. "Your heavenly Father feedeth
them . . . will He not much more feed you?"

That is beautiful poetry, says the sophisticated col-
legian, but you must not ask me to believe that God takes
notice of each individual of the human race and knows
each by name. And yet, as Dr. Ralph Sockman has said,
"If from the print of my finger-tip the FBI can identify
me though I bury myself in the millions of London or the
wastes of Sahara, why should it be thought a thing in-
credible that our heavenly Father should know the man
He has created with such individual marks?"

That does not mean that we are to fall back into idle,
wishful musing, saying, Very well, then, I shall be cared
for — why should I worry? The bird which the heavenly
Father feeds works as if its life depended on it. Every
flower is the product of an intricate, co-ordinated labora-
tory with thousands of cells pumping up moisture from
the earth and converting the energy of the sun into color
and fragrance. Faith does not mean inaction. What it
anchors in is the sure order of the Father's world. "While
the earth remaineth, seedtime and harvest, and cold and
heat, and summer and winter, and day and night, shall not
cease." We have made the first station of faith when we
have discovered the boundaries of the faith-world.

Faith forbids anxiety. There will be hardships and disappointments, but they touch only the surface of life.
Into the deep centers where we have our relation of fellowship with God they cannot penetrate; and they should
not, therefore, disturb the Christian's quietness of mind.

We have a double armor against anxiety: we know God as our Father; and we know that His providence extends to "the grass of the field." We are without excuse for lack of faith; for the Christian, unbelief is treason. We must first destroy what Jesus has taught us of God before we may ask for sympathy in our doubts. Faith is the magic wand that turns night into day, gloom into gladness, despondency into hope

> I know not what the future hath
> Of marvel or surprise,
> Assured alone that life and death
> His mercy underlies.
>
> .   .   .   .   .   .
>
> I know not where His islands lift
> Their fronded palms in air;
> I only know I cannot drift
> Beyond His love and care.

Whittier called the poem from which those lines are taken "The Eternal Goodness." He might have called it simply "Faith."

To every thing there is a season, and a time to every purpose under heaven: . . . a time to keep silence, and a time to speak.

Ecclesiastes 3:1 and 7

9
Speech and Silence

IN THAT most comprehensive time table, the third chapter of Ecclesiastes, the wise man says, "There is a time to keep silence, and a time to speak." Each is true of personal religion. There is a time to speak, a time for the clear, courageous word of testimony; and there is a time also to keep silence, a time when silence is the answer of wisdom, of faith, and of hope. There are these two extremes in Christian experience, and the golden mean of wisdom discovers when "silence is golden," and when "a word fitly spoken is like apples of gold in vessels of silver."

In many respects speech is man's crowning attribute. By language we reflect all that the senses perceive and the mind conceives. "The older I grow," wrote Thomas Carlyle near the end of his life, "the more I feel the wisdom of the answer of the Catechism, 'the chief end of man is to glorify God.'" He was thinking of speech and confessions of faith. "Ye shall be my witnesses." The first function of a witness is to speak. What a mighty testimony the first Christians gave in speech! Our Gospels were the first Christian testimony, and since their day we have multiplied our confessions of faith into libraries.

In our day we have seen a revival of the testimony of speech, perhaps to the point of becoming suspicious of it. In another mood Carlyle said, "All speech is short-lived, foolish and untrue; the dumb nations are the builders of the world." But, one has said, he made us dissatisfied with speech by talking so much himself — forty volumes of it. But silence does not have a monopoly of virtue. "Morning by morning," said Isaiah, "he wakeneth mine ear to hear as they that are taught," but also "He hath made my mouth to be a sharp sword." It was said of the late Dr. Maltbie Babcock, a clergyman very popular with men and much sought as a speaker at their assemblies, that whenever the talk would become loose or questionable, he would leave the company with the words, "You must excuse me, but I have a previous engagement with my Master." It is doubtful whether, in our personal religion, we have suffered more remorse from speech than from silence, the silence that was not ignorance or disdain, but cowardice and falsehood and base consent to evil. Who of us can look back upon his past life, however lowly or limited, without failing to see that again and again his worst sin was silence? Let us recall the times when, under the call to confession and prayer, our lips proved traitors to our hearts; the times when through our cowardice to bear witness we denied the truth; the times when we were too weak to protest against baseless slander; the times when we failed to speak forth the reason for the hope that was in us, though our heart was full; the times when we were silent before the ignorant or the dying, or before questioning children or a troubled friend. Our own remissness is sufficient to justify Carlyle's words, "If the word is not there, you have no man there either."

But if there is a time to speak, there is also a time to keep silence. Silence is the answer of wisdom when we stand face to face with the mysteries of God. There is the mystery of His being. Who can tell what God is, or give body to the great divine Spirit? At best we can but speak of Him in terms of our own finite personality. We speak of His voice, His ear, His hand, but we admit that these are but anthropomorphisms. Like Moses we see only God's "back" — the experience of His presence as He passes by. There is the mystery of His ways with men, the profound mystery of His silence in the face of our suffering. One of the deepest woes of the psalmists was the intolerable tension of that silence. "Hold not thy peace at my tears, for I am a stranger with thee." Like Job, their concern was not vindication but that they lose not the God in whom they believed. In *Les Miserables* Victor Hugo, speaking of that incomparably good man, Bishop Myriel, says: "He was one of those men who could sit for a whole hour beside a man who had lost his wife — and say nothing." There are psalms that seem to see God sitting by the side of His saints and letting them pray themselves into comfort.

There is the mystery of life. Who knows its origin, or who can trace the secret processes of its growth? There is the mystery of death. Why must good men go to their reward through the humiliation of physical dissolution? There is the mystery of our personal consciousness — a clod of clay, a reed shaken in the wind, yet singing to itself:

> I am God's temple. In my breast
> Where beats my helpless, hurrying heart
> That at such futile joys will start
> And stop because death's hand is pressed
> Too close, He dwells, my royal guest.

In the face of such mysteries it is the part of wisdom to keep silence until God bids us speak.

Silence is also the answer of faith. Confessions of faith were meant to be spoken, but in personal religion there is more faith in honest silence than in half our words. When like Job we have been stripped of all that makes life dear, the answer of faith is that of the psalmist, "I was dumb; I opened not my mouth, because thou didst it." When Job's dialectics failed, he found God in silent wonder. Faith is silence without denial when one does not know what to say.

Silence is also the language of hope. There are some things that do not lend themselves to words; hope is one of them. Hope is the silent anchor of the soul; it lies too deep for words. It is peculiarly a Christian virtue; it grew out of the early experience of recovery when all seemed lost. But unless hope is rooted in experience it is mere wishful musing. The ground of our hope is Jesus Christ. What is the ground of our hope that this world will yet be made a worthy footstool for our Master's feet, that those for whom we pray may yet find their way to God, that we ourselves shall yet behold our Lord in His glory? Unless this hope is anchored in the confidence that He who brought again from the dead the Lord Jesus, the great Shepherd of the sheep, will also with Him freely give us all things, it is delusion. Christian hope knows where its anchor rests, and that anchor holds.

And with Him perished all that men hold most dear;
Hope lay beside Him in the sepulchre,

Love grew corse cold, and all things beautiful beside
  Died when He died.

  He rose!

And with Him hope arose, and life and light.
Men said, "Not Christ but Death died yesternight."
And joy and truth and all things virtuous
  Rose when He rose.

As for me, I will call upon God; and the Lord shall save me.

Evening, and morning, and at noon, will I pray, and cry aloud: and he shall hear my voice.

Psalm 55:16-17

10
Prayer

As for me, says God, I know nothing so beautiful in the whole
    world
As a mere child having a talk with the good Lord
At the bottom of the garden;
Asking questions and giving the answers himself (it's safer that
    way).
A little man telling the good Lord about his woes,
As seriously as anyone in the world,
And comforting himself as if the good Lord were comforting
    him.
But let me tell you that those words of comfort which he says to
    himself
Come straight and properly from me.[1]

Our little grandson, aged four, is wrestling with the
concept of God. It is a staggering experience. God cannot be seen, yet He can hear. He is outside us, and He is
within us. Is it God speaking in the thunder that rolls
over the hills, and in the sigh that wells from his mother's
throat? Is it God who receives the offerings at the altar
and who answers the questions we put to Him in the
garden?

The little man has the first concept of personal religion.
He wants to know and he wants to help — help God. He
talks to God as he talks to himself.

So natural an instinct as prayer should have natural
expression. Children have it; why have we adults made

---

[1] C. Péguy, *God Speaks*, Pantheon, Inc., New York.

it so artificial? We so strive to clothe God with majesty that we have well-nigh lost Him as our heavenly Father. Why can we not be as childlike in our prayers as in our faith? In fact, words are not necessary in personal prayer.

> Prayer is the soul's sincere desire,
> Uttered or unexpressed.

"And in praying do not heap up empty phrases as the Gentiles do; for they think they will be heard for their many words." Jesus did not give His disciples His prayer as a ritual but as an illustration of what the right attitude to God would lead them to desire and as an explanation of His own seasons of communion with the Father. Prayer is not an end in itself, but a means to an end, the discovery of the divine will, the enlistment of the divine help, self-dedication to the divine purpose. There are proprieties in prayer — adoration, confession, thanksgiving, supplication — and one does well to observe them, particularly in public prayer. But in the prayers of the Bible one is struck by the directness with which the suppliant comes to his need and the intimate urgency of his appeals. Jeremiah's confessions and the Psalms are the best types of personal prayer. At times those saints literally remonstrate with God. For prayer is the indicator of our inmost interests. When a man is intensely in earnest he does not wait for times or seasons, or rubrics or postures. Abraham made his prayer for Lot standing where he was. Jacob prayed as he wrestled with an unseen foe, Deborah prayed as she sat beneath her palm tree, Solomon communed with God in his dreams and asked for wisdom. Isaiah prayed as he stood in the temple court, Jeremiah prayed in the stocks in the gate of Benjamin. Daniel prayed in the lions' den. Jesus prayed as He reclined with His disciples at the last supper, and on His knees in the garden, and on the cross with the nails pinioning His hands and feet. We have sentimentally centered our thought of the praying Christ too exclusively on the figure of Jesus in Gethsemane, after Hofmann's classic picture. It is the Jesus with a will and a purpose who has been the inspiration of our Western Christianity, the Jesus of Sallman's matchless head, not the Christ on His knees, but the Christ on His feet. That type of strong man prays — let there be no mistake about it — but he prays as he works. When Luther said he was so busy that he had to pray three hours a day, he was not on his knees but at his desk. When the janitor at the Wartburg overheard his prayer, "Lord, matters stand between us as before," he was finishing up a knotty piece of translation. Oliver Cromwell and John Wesley prayed in the saddle, Florence Nightingale in the hospital tent, Howard Kelly in the operating room, Father Heyer in his house-wagon in the Minnesota hills or in his ox-cart on the India trails.

We have been having a revival of interest in Brother Lawrence's *Practice of the Presence of God*. Would that with a revival of interest in his devotion we might have a revival of his saintly common sense! In his conversations he said it was a great delusion to think that the times of prayer ought to differ from other times; that we are as strictly obliged to adhere to God by action in the time of action as by prayer in the season of prayer . . . that when the appointed time of prayer was past, he found no difference because he still continued with God, praising and blessing Him with all his might, so that he passed his life in continual joy. "The time of business," said he, "does not differ from the time of prayer, and in the noise and clatter of my kitchen, while several persons are at the same time calling for different things, I possess God in as great tranquility as if I were upon my knees at the Blessed Sacrament." [2]

------

[2] *Brother Lawrence: His Letters and Conversations on the Practice of the Presence of God*, Forward Movement, Cincinnati, Ohio.

But be doers of the word, and not hearers only, deceiving yourselves.

James 1:22
(from the Revised Standard Version of the New Testament)

11

Conduct, the Badge of Personal Religion

JESUS CHRIST created the Christian Church. Today it is the greatest single institution in the world. Six hundred million souls profess allegiance to it. The sun never sets on its shrines. And yet Jesus created no outward framework of the Church. He wrote no constitution for it, He left no ritual of initiation and stated assemblies. He made no manual of personal habits, He established no ascetic order, prescribed no distinctive garb, sought no national home for His followers. He left no insignia save the Cross on which He died. He simply lifted His followers to the high plane of children of God. He put the badge of their membership in His Church on that high level. He told them that they were the light of the world. Light is a guide for the feet which would otherwise stumble in the darkness. That is what Jesus' followers were to be, emulating His example (John 8:12). He told them they were the salt of the earth. What salt is, in the midst of the things in which it is placed, Jesus' followers were to be to those who inhabit "the earth." It seasons, purifies, preserves, even tends to change the character of what is salted. If salt has lost these saving qualities, it is worthless and is cast out.

In figures such as these Jesus told His followers what their responsibility was. We find it echoed in the Epistles. In his letter to Titus Paul admonishes that they who have believed in God be careful to maintain "good works."

Paul does not mean, as a careful reading of the letter shows, the giving of money, food, clothing, tracts and the like, but that the aged men "be sober, grave, temperate, sound in faith, in charity." The aged women likewise are admonished that they "be in behavior as becometh holiness, not gossips, not given to much wine . . . that they may teach the young women to be sober, to love their husbands . . . discreet, chaste, keepers at home. . . ." All these homely things, common or secular virtues, are included in what the Apostle calls "good works."

It must have been humiliating to the Apostle Paul that in his letters to the churches which he had established he had to speak so often and so specifically about the conduct of the individual members. It would seem that the high privilege of the New Covenant would bind us with a gentleman's agreement to a type of life in the likeness of Jesus Christ. Making all allowance for the drag of our human nature which causes us daily to stumble, it is a question whether Christians now, any more than in the days of the Apostles, seriously weigh the relation of their conduct to their profession of faith. "Conduct," as one of the apostles of the nineteenth century was fond of saying, "is three-fourths of life." It is that because at least three-fourths of our life is lived in contact with other people. Conduct is the common language of self-disclosure. "What you are speaks so loud I cannot hear what you say."

Conduct, moreover, must have a standard. The Christian standard of conduct is Christ. From the days of the Apostles to our own, the test question to apply to our acts is, What would Jesus do? One of the most needed recoveries to be made by the Christian of our day is the religious conception of life which marked the early Christians. Every relation of their lives was glorified by the new relation with Christ. As unto Him the farmer tilled the soil, the merchant watched his weights, the baker molded his loaf, the boatman plied his oars, the servant performed his tasks. It is true that much of the diligence of those early Christians was inspired by the expectation of an early return of their Lord, but Christ is as near to us as He was to the saints on the Judean hills. Out of such a sense of relationship with Christ came the inspiration of George Herbert's lines

> Who sweeps a room as for Thy laws
> Makes that and the action fine.

We have had a revival of it in such little books as *Hiram Goff, Shoemaker by the Grace of God; What Would Jesus Do?* and the recovery of *Brother Lawrence: His Letters and Conversations on the Practice of the Presence of God.*

We are calling upon the church for a revival of personal evangelism. There could be no more effective appeal to the unchurched than a revival of the imitation of Christ within the churches. The world is still sensitive to "good works." A godly life is never misunderstood, never discounted, never denied. Conduct is the badge of personal religion.

And keep your conscience clear, so that, when you are abused, those who revile your good behavior in Christ may be put to shame.

I Peter 3:16
(from the Revised Standard Version
of the New Testament)

12
A Good Conscience

WHATEVER else personal religion is, it is striving to have a good conscience toward God and toward man. The word conscience occurs thirty times in the New Testament, all of them in the Epistles (except in the doubtful passage including John 8:9). The word does not occur in the Old Testament, but, while the word is missing, the thing is there. It is a voice, a mysterious voice, the voice of God speaking to the soul. Adam seeks to hide himself in the midst of the trees of the garden, and the Voice asks, "Where art thou?" Cain has lured his brother into the field and slain him, and the Voice asks, "Where is Abel thy brother?" Saul has taken for his own the dedicated things of God, and the Voice asks, "What meaneth this bleating of sheep in mine ears?" David has committed a deadly and undiscovered crime, and the Voice cries out, "Thou art the man."

Conscience is also called a palate, a moral palate by which we are able instinctively to taste differences in character and conduct. Without conscience all things would taste alike morally. The thing we call falsehood would taste just like the thing called truth, and the thing we call hate would taste just like the thing we call love. We have this God-given moral sense that we may chart our way, but we may tamper with the delicate faculty until it becomes unreliable. "The light of the body is the eye. If therefore thine eye be single (sound), thy whole body shall be full of light; but if thine eye be evil (not sound), thy whole body shall be full of darkness." Conscience may be disobeyed until its voice becomes faint or ceases to speak. Herod could not get a word out of Christ, though he asked Him many questions, because for years he would not hear His voice; and conscience, like the Lord of conscience, ceases to speak after men have too long neglected its warnings. Sailing out of Boston harbor in a driving storm, guided in the difficult channel by many lights and buoys, we came at last to a bell-buoy with its clapper gone. There it was, riding on the waves whose swells should have sent its warning peals out into the gloom, but now as mute as the grave. It was a symbol of conscience when men have robbed it of its tongue.

Our consciences need to be kept in good repair. They need to be kept sharp at the edge. It is nice work they have to do, and many a hard knot lies in their way. Years ago I daily passed a village blacksmith who earned his livelihood by sharpening stonecutters' tools. Knowing that his work was limited to two employers, and yet finding him busy every day over a pile of chisels, I asked how often each needed sharpening. Looking up in surprise, he said: "Every day! It's hard stone they cut." How much more careful men are of their tools than of their consciences! Let self-examination before the light of truth lapse, and soon our consciences become dull, and then smooth, and finally they polish the surface they were meant to cut. If we neglect conscience, or turn a deaf ear to it, it will soon cease to speak at all. Swiss watch-makers devised a phosphorescent dial by means of which the faces of watches are illuminated in darkness and become visible at ordinary distances. Every few days, however, the watch must be exposed to the sunlight, or the phosphorescence fails and the time can no longer be ascertained in the darkness. Conscience is an illuminated dial to be eagerly scanned in dark and perplexing days; but it gives clear and true direction only while it is kept animated by the light of heaven.

Conscience is our arbiter, the supreme arbiter before which every thought must be brought into the captivity of obedience, but conscience itself must bow to the light of heaven. Its final appeal is not to itself but to the Word of God. "I have often thought," says Dr. J. H. Jowett, "that the apportionment of the ancient city of Edinburgh is a fair and fitting symbol of every healthy and well-ordered life. There, in the lower part of the city, are the highways of commerce, the channels of trade. A little higher are the well-cultivated gardens into which a wearied body can turn for recreation and rest. Still higher are the colleges and seats of learning, where students burrow into ancient lore to enrich a present mind. And high above all there towers the gray old castle, and in the topmost part of the castle stands the time-gun, which every day roars out the royal time, the standard time, the standard to which the clocks are adjusted in the seats of learning and down in the centers of trade. It is to me a symbol of a healthy and well-governed life, in which all the varied activities of trade and mind and recreation are adjusted to the royal proclamation of the Conscience, enthroned on high above them all."

Satis viatici ad coelum — *Enough money
to get to heaven with.*

Archbishop Warham

13
Stewardship

WE GIVE expression to our religion in a variety of ways, not least in our use of the things with which we are endowed, and in nothing more certainly than in our attitude to and our use of money. The Book of Proverbs and the Epistle of James, both of them thesauruses on personal religion, make the use of money co-ordinate with our use of speech. Money is the circulating medium of commercial exchange. In a sense it has only the value we give it. For the majority of us our chief concern is to secure enough for our needs. It is a question whether it is a greater peril for those who possess it than for those who must struggle for it.

"It is very evident," says Henry David Thoreau, addressing the general reader, "what kind of lives the most of you live . . . always on the limits, trying to get into business and trying to get out of debt, a very ancient slough, called by the Latins *aes alienum* (another's brass, for some of their coins were made of brass), still living and dying and buried by another's brass, promising to pay tomorrow and dying today, insolvent, seeking to curry favor, to get custom by how many modes, only not state-prison offenses, lying, flattering, voting, contracting yourselves into a nut-shell of civility, or dilating into an atmosphere of thin and vaporous generosity that you may persuade your neighbor to let you make his shoes, or his hat, or his coat, or his carriage, or to import his groceries for him, making yourselves sick that you may make what you call a living. . . . The mass of men live lives of quiet desperation." [1]

That is the kind of temptation money subjects us to if we do not have it. Is it worse or better to have it? Is the peril of covetousness greater or less than the peril of possession? It determined the destiny of the rich young ruler seeking to know what he must do to inherit eternal life. He has had many successors.

Sir James M. Barrie has left us a picture in his play, "The Will," for which the original might have sat yesterday. The scene is a lawyers' office. A young couple have come to make a will. The husband has a thousand dollars, and his salary is eight hundred dollars. The young wife is in tears at the thought of it. But the young husband is firm — it is a man's duty. And they agree that he shall make provision for two dependent cousins, and that fifty dollars is to go to the hospital. The will is drawn up accordingly, and duly signed; and the young couple depart with an air of elation. When they have gone the lawyers exchange glances and smile.

Twenty years pass, and they are again in the lawyers' office. This time the wife is present not by invitation but by insistence. There is no mention of dependent cousins or the hospital. The husband is now worth one hundred thousand dollars, and his wife is the sole beneficiary. They leave, but not in elation. And again the lawyers exchange glances and smile.

_____

[1] *Walden*, Chap. I.

Twenty years more pass. An old man comes to the lawyers' office — alone. He is now Sir Philip Ross. His wife is dead, and his only son is dead, killed in a brawl, while his only daughter has eloped with the chauffeur. He comes to make his will; he is now a millionaire, but he is bitter and miserable. He directs his lawyers to make equal distribution among six men whose gold he has won in the game of business. "With my curse." [2]

There is but one of two things to be done with this tyrant, Money; either — master it in stewardship, or be mastered by it. "It will be hard for a rich man to enter into the kingdom of heaven."

> If thou art rich, thou art poor;
> For like an ass whose back with ingots bows,
> Thou boastest thy heavy riches but a journey,
> And death unloads thee.

No, we cannot take it with us; but it may be so used in this world as to be a blessing here and a joy hereafter. George Peabody was a millionaire, but it was his daily prayer that he might be enabled to use his wealth for the good of his fellow-men. That sentence was carved on his gravestone, and his name is still a blessing to thousands. By our use of our "unrighteous mammon" we may make an entrance into "eternal habitation." It will not open the gates of heaven to us — only Christ is the door — but it can give us what Peter in his second letter calls "an abundant entrance." No joy can be greater than that of being welcomed by those who will say: "We were

---

[2] *The Plays of James M. Barrie,* Charles Scribner's Sons, New York.

hungry and you gave us food; we were thirsty and you gave us drink; we were strangers and you welcomed us; we were naked and you clothed us; we were in prison and you came unto us." *"Satis viatici ad coelum"* — "Enough money to get to heaven with," said the dying Archbishop Warham when his servant told him he had left but thirty pounds. He had bartered his silver and gold for the widow's gratitude, the orphan's love, and the poor man's prayer. He had made friends who would receive him into eternal habitations.

. . . I haven't a conviction I'm not willing to die for.

General Hawley

14
Conviction

MR. AARON HARTER, a sturdy layman of the last generation, who himself had quite positive convictions, was wont to rally audiences to a clear-cut allegiance to their faith by relating the story of a farmer in the Harrisburg market who had two large stone jars, one of "smearkase" and the other of apple butter, but only one dipper, which he used alternately in drawing out the contents of both, until one could not tell which was "smearkase" and which was apple butter. "So it is," Mr. Harter would conclude, "with many so-called Christians. You can't tell whether they belong more to Christ or to the world."

There is no more sorry figure in the world than "Mr. Facing-both-ways." He is not only unsatisfactory to all with whom he has to do, but he is unsatisfactory to himself.

There was once a famous rabbi-judge of Chelem who was noted for his impartiality. Two litigants came to him one day to settle their dispute. After listening long and patiently to the plaintiff, the judge said to him, "I think you are in the right." The plaintiff left in high spirits. "But," exclaimed the defendant, "you have not heard my side of the case." Whereupon the judge listened with equal patience to him, and at the conclusion of his argument said to him, "I think you are in the right." But the judge's wife, who had been eavesdropping, was puzzled. "How is it possible," she said to her husband, "that they should both be in the right?" The judge pondered the question long and deeply. Finally he turned to his wife and said, "I think you are in the right." [1]

We may retain a temporary popularity by agreeing with both sides of a controversy, but sooner or later we come to grief and are despised in our own households, if not in our own souls. Truth and falsehood, fact and fiction, cannot be equally right. "Woe unto them that call evil good, and good evil; that put darkness for light and light for darkness" (Isa. 5:20). These things are not alternatives.

A recent writer in *The Hibbert Journal* speaks of "Alternate Assumptions in Christian Teaching." Christian *teaching* is a matter of conviction, and conviction rests on evidence. It is not to be confused with bigotry. Bigotry is religious zeal run mad. Conviction is a deliberate judgment based on testimony. Such evidence may be either presumptive or factual. "The bigot," says Oliver Wendell Holmes, "is like the pupil of the eye; the more light you put upon it, the more it will contract." Bigotry is the defense mechanism of ignorance. As a French littérateur once put it, "Conviction is the conscience of the mind." It is intelligence plus will. "We did not follow cleverly devised myths when we made known unto you the power and coming of our Lord Jesus Christ, but we were eyewitnesses of his majesty" (II Pet. 1:16, RSV). That testimony would stand in any court.

---

[1] *The Wisdom of Israel*, By Lewis Browne, Random House, New York, 1945.

A Christian ought to be able — and willing — to give a reason for the hope that is in him. "Conscience," says Shakespeare, "does make cowards of us all." But conscience does more; it lifts us above all other fear. It lifted Peter above the misery and suspicion of denial to the courage that enabled him to say to his judges, "Whether it be right in the sight of God to listen to you rather than to God, you must judge; for we cannot but speak of what we have seen and heard." A Christian ought not to be concerned about what man, even a Caesar, may think of him, or be worried about the consequences of his decisions; his concern should be to be loyal to the truth.

Dr. C. C. Morrison has been at pains to point out in *The Christian Century* the weaknesses of Protestantism. Undoubtedly one of them is Protestant testimony, both in teaching and preaching. We miss the note, not of certainty — that is a matter of objective determination — but of conviction, which is a matter of subjective loyalty. We miss the glowing surrender of a vacillating Peter to the evangel which had fulfilled his nation's hopes. We miss the fearless testimony of a Paul before Agrippa that "this Jesus," whom the leaders of his people and the Romans had put to death, was alive and had appeared to him with commanding power. We miss the flaming shafts of a Savonarola's indictment of his beloved city and its corrupt aristocracy. We miss the stubborn protest of a Luther before the pomp and officialdom of a world empire, "My conscience is bound by the word of God. I cannot and will not recant." We miss the singing arrows of a Whitefield shot from the bow of the deep conviction of the mortal sickness of sin, and the divine remedy of grace, piercing the armor of self-complacency and causing men to cry out once more, "What must I do to be saved?"

When General Hawley, a United States Senator from Connecticut, opposed the opening of the gates of the Centennial Exhibition in 1876 on Sunday, he was met with the sneer, "Sentiment, sentiment." "Not sentiment, but conviction," replied the general, "and I haven't a conviction I'm not willing to die for." That was the spirit that made a great soldier. Why can we not carry the same conviction into the issues of peace? Vacillation never won a convert — or saved one's own soul.

I have a little army of faculties to which the will has to be the inspiring and pervading commandant.

J. H. Jowett

15
Strengthening the Will

WHEN General Hawley said he hadn't a conviction he was not willing to die for, he added something to his conviction. Conviction is a judicial process. In itself it is merely a judgment. To be effective in personal religion, it must be reinforced by the will. The will is the driving force of personality. It is the executive agent of the soul, the commanding officer of all the faculties. "I have a little army of faculties," said Dr. J. H. Jowett, "to which the will has to be the inspiring and pervading commandant." If the will is strong, all the faculties will respond with alacrity and precision and carry a man to victory over all ramparts of opposition. If the will is weak, the most brilliant faculties will be like a demoralized army not knowing who is in command or whether there is any commander. Why should a Corsican interloper or an Austrian house painter shake all Europe to its foundations, while the darling of a vicarage and of two universities, a poet and a philosopher, be the victim of narcotics and the charge of charity? The answer is the difference between an indomitable will and a vacillating will.

When we ask why one man should have a strong will and another a weak will we are face to face with one of life's imponderables. Paul found it a still greater mystery that two men should reside in the same body. "I am," he says in substance (in that illuminating bit of autobiography in Romans 7), "two men, a low man and a high man, a man of the flesh and a man of the Spirit, a dead man and a living man. And these two men are myself. And there is a conflict going on. The dead man drags me down, the living man lifts me up; the desires of the flesh pull me back, the desires of the Spirit push me forward. I am drawn in opposite directions by conflicting wills. O wretched man that I am, who shall deliver me from this contradiction?" It is plain that help must come from outside. You may have read the story of the Siberian prisoner in the mines, chained to a comrade who died. For days he was in bondage to a dead man. There was no deliverance for him until the keeper of the prison released him. Paul was like that. "Who shall deliver me?"

If Paul had lived in our day his friends might have sent him to a psychiatrist. And that would have interested him. He would have been told that he had a discordant personality; that what he needed was to have his personality integrated. It was so disintergrated that the lower elements of the self were waging successful conflict with the higher elements. What he needed was a unifying principle of life. And Paul had his answer: "I have found it; I thank my God through Jesus Christ." It was not a principle but a Person. He had been in bondage to a person — himself, the lust of the flesh to which he was chained. Someone stronger than he must take command of him. He must surrender his life to a higher Will. If he was to be a slave, he would be a slave to the Highest. He was not restored to his old self, renovated and improved; he became a new creature. The carnal man had to die; the spiritual man had to be born. That meant that the new and higher Will had to take command of the shattered forces of his faculties. "For the law of the Spirit of life in Christ Jesus has set me free from the law of sin and death." "And the life which I now live in the flesh I live by the faith (fellowship) of the Son of God, who loved me, and gave himself for me."

In the battle of Marengo the Austrians considered the day won. The French army was inferior in numbers and had given way under the Austrian assaults, Austrian divisions extended to the right and the left. Then, though to the French the battle seemed lost, Napoleon himself took command and ordered the Old Guard to charge down the center. The spirit of Napoleon took possession of the wavering troops who now turned the battle into an Austrian rout. Chapter 7 of Romans has been called a spiritual Marengo. Paul at first seems to be speaking of a losing battle; but just as his spirit was about to sink in despair, he sensed the presence of Jesus Christ at his side. Here was the Will that turned defeat into victory.

Such a victory is not won by a mere passive surrender. Surrender to Christ is not passivity. It is very active enlistment. It is the rallying of every power of the soul and bringing every thought into the captivity of obedience to Christ. We lose ourselves in Him. His will is now supreme. All our various associations, each with their own motives and activities, are now taken up and unified in that one all-pervading loyalty. We follow Him. And because, as we Christians hold, that Will is the revelation of the soul, of the integrated soul of the world, our lives will be integrated and made complete in Him.

*The misfortunes hardest to bear are those
that never happen.*

James Russell Lowell

16
Good Cheer

A COROLLARY of faith is good cheer. It is our Christian duty to "be of good cheer." The words are our Lord's. They close the announcement to the Twelve in His farewell to them in the Upper Room. He was about to leave them. What greater misfortune could befall them? And yet He bade them "be of good cheer." That is the way He bids us who claim to be His followers face our disappointments. We shall later recall the ground upon which we can "be of good cheer." It is enough now for us to know that that is what He expects of us. It is the Christian attitude toward life.

If doing were as easy as saying, all men would "be of good cheer" — but we know that they are not. Worry is the robber baron that preys upon rich and poor, high and low. Navigators say that all ships leak a little, and if their crews were to give all attention to the possibilities that lurk behind a leak they might never bring their ships to port. All souls have their worries. The test of our religion is, what are we doing with the worries that come our way?

Jesus said, "Be of good cheer." The verb is imperative. It is something we can do. We can put our faith to work. It is a matter of the will.

> The mind is its own place, and in itself
> Can shape a heaven of hell, a hell of heaven.

It is a common delusion that our happiness is determined

by circumstances. That were deliberately to invite unhappiness, for no man's circumstances are quite satisfactory. Envy is the demon of our undoing here. As long as we fix our eyes on others' circumstances we invite unhappiness. We still cling to the old Hebrew idea that happiness means material success, the reward of keeping the Law. That is the age-old fallacy with which the writer of Psalm 73 wrestled. He was surrounded by far less conscientious men who prospered in every material way. They had more than heart could wish. Their eyes stood out with fatness in well-fed comfort. They never had need to "tighten their belt." They were free from the ills which come from poverty and sickness. They made suffering goodness the butt of their coarse jeers. They blasphemed heaven by their insolence. The psalmist had taken the prosperous worldlings at their own appraisal, and, measured by their yardstick, he was vindicated in his unhappiness. In his discouragement he had all but given up the case for religion.

His feet had almost slipped, he tells us, when he decided to leave his brooding-pen and go into the house of God. How different things looked there! His prosperous neighbors, whose cold disdain had so hurt his soul, shriveled to their true size. He saw, not what he had missed but what he had escaped. And now he was overwhelmed with self-reproach. He had been a "beast" before God. He had been like the elder brother in the parable of the Prodigal Son, to whom the father said, "Son, thou art ever with me, and all that I have is thine." He had forgotten the things which God exalts. He now discerned that his house was built upon a rock. The demon of envy had fled.

Another demon of unhappiness is fear. It is a harder demon to fight. It is a form of borrowed trouble. Of all forms of worry, none is more pernicious than this, because it wastes both soul and body over evils which never come to pass. How true are Lowell's words, "The misfortunes hardest to bear are those that never happen." The ills which most of us fear are many times worse than those we actually bear. Fear creates worry, and worry induces fear, thus forging a vicious circle that binds its victim with bands of steel. Fear is ever looking backward, calling up specters that will not rest. Worrying over the past will never change it, but if like St. George we slay our dragon fear, we have already changed our future. Our shield is faith with which we can quench the fiery darts of the evil one. Faith is the victory over fear. "Happy is the man that maketh the Lord his trust." His victory is already won.

In one of the thrilling stories of recent years a man, crossing an abandoned coal field in Cornwall, England, in the night in search of his nephew who was lost, fell into an apparently bottomless pit, but he saved himself by grasping a projecting beam, to which he clung with every ounce of his will through the slow-moving hours of darkness. At daybreak he found that his feet were but a scant yard from a solid platform. It is a parable of Providence.

> Deep in unfathomable mines
> Of never-failing skill

He treasures up His bright designs
And works His sovereign will.

Ye fearful saints! fresh courage take;
The clouds ye so much dread
Are big with mercy and shall break
In blessings on your head.

*Temptation includes whatever presents
an opportunity of choice between good
and evil, and that is the picture of the
whole arena of life.*

Newman Hall

17
Temptation

TEMPTATION is a good word with a bad history. "God cannot be tempted with evil, neither tempteth he any man." And yet "lead us not into temptation" is a petition in the Lord's Prayer. It is one of the common marks of our experience that we are subject to temptation from the beginning to the end of our lives. "There hath no temptation taken you but such as is common to man." Because we are human we shall never be free from its persistent assaults. "Every man is tempted when he is drawn away of his own lusts and enticed."

The word "temptation" comes from a very good verbal family, from the Hebrew down. It means "to stretch, or test by stretching." Leather is tested over the hoop of a drum; men are tested over the rim of their freedom. What curious kaleidoscopes words make! To try is to tempt, and to probe is to prove. It is one of the oldest formulas of human speech that life is a probation. To probe a wound is to test the character of it. Our life is a probing, a probating. "Temptation includes whatever presents an opportunity of choice between good and evil," says Dr. Newman Hall, "and that is the picture of the whole arena of life." Life is a necessary and perpetual testing in the process of its development. A man may be put to the test for a good purpose or a bad purpose. It is only in the former sense that we may speak of God's tempting us.

It is unfortunate that the word has lingered only in its bad sense. God does not mean that we are to fall in temptation — or, if we do, that we are never to rise again; but we are expected to "do our part." In this, as in all other elements of the spiritual life; "we are workers together with God."

God expects us to heed the instincts of peril with which He has endowed us. A bank teller was asked whether she was never anxious lest she should let a counterfeit bill pass undetected. "At first," she replied, "but my examiner told me, 'Do not worry, for the first time you touch bad paper you will feel a shiver as though you had received an electric shock.'" Conscience is our instinct of peril. If we heed it we have taken the first step in overcoming temptation.

The second step is to keep clear the issue involved in the temptation. This involves calling things by their right names. "Woe unto them that call evil good, and good evil" (Isa. 5:20). It is in the secret place of the soul that it is so easy to yield to self-sophistication; and it is just there that the issue of the battle is to be decided. It was when Eve began to doubt that evil was evil that she prepared the way to her fall. In a powerful and eloquent lecture delivered during the Battle of Britain by Emeritus Professor McNeile Dixon (quoted in the *Expository Times*), he said: "When I find myself at any of the famous cross roads of thought, where the darkness thickens and decisions are hard, I retire for my encouragement upon certain convictions, fixed stars in my little firmament. . . . Here is an instance. Whatever men are

minded to call them, I continue to believe that deceit
remains deceit, cruelty cruelty, treachery treachery, kindness kindness, as certainly as food is food, and poison
poison, and that villainy, however successful, is still villainy." In the hour of temptation this is precisely what
we must do — keep the issue clear.

Equally we must keep clear the truth that no man
lives unto himself — or falls unto himself. In "Sand, Wind
and Stars" the French aviator St. Exupéry tells how he
and a comrade crashed in the Sahara and wandered about
aimlessly for hours. They were on the verge of utter
collapse, their uppermost desire being simply to fall down
in the sand and sleep. Then he tells how he was able to
resist that overwhelming desire: "I was haunted by a
vision of my wife's eyes under the halo of her hat. Of her
face I could see only the eyes, questioning me and looking
at me earnestly and yearningly. 'I am answering with all
my strength,' I would cry out. I was perfectly ready to
fall asleep, whether for a night or for eternity . . . ; but
that cry, the cry that would be set up in my home, that
great desolation — that was what I could not bear." [1]
And it saved him.

But, supremely, we must keep in mind that we are not
our own, we are bought with a price. There is another
Face, there are other Eyes upon us in our temptations.
"We have not an high priest that cannot be touched with
the feeling of our infirmities, but one that in all points has

---

[1] "Sand, Wind and Stars," in *Airman's Odyssey*, Reynal & Hitchcock,
New York.

been tempted like as we are, yet without sin." He knows the battle we wage and the foe we face, and "His touch hath still its ancient power."

> In the hour of trial,
> Jesus, plead for me,
> Lest by base denial,
> I depart from Thee;
> When Thou seest me waver,
> With a look recall,
> Nor for fear or favor
> Suffer me to fall.
>
> With forbidden pleasures
> Should this vain world charm,
> Or its tempting treasures
> Spread, to work me harm,
> Bring to my remembrance
> Sad Gethsemane,
> Or, in darker semblance,
> Cross-crowned Calvary.

We are like the weaver who plies his shuttle and fills in the web, thread by thread, making a pattern we do not see. We work on the wrong side, like him, and do not see what to all others is clear.

18
Character

THERE is no element of personal religion about which we should be more concerned than our character. Character is commonly understood as the thing a man essentially is, the qualities which make up his personality. As a matter of fact, it is a man's distinguishing mark in comparison with others. "Character" is a Greek word, which occurs only once in the New Testament, namely, in Hebrews 1:3, in the classic description of Jesus. The writer says, "He is the express image of his (God's) person" (AV), or "the impress of his substance" (ARV mg), or "stamped with God's own character" (Moffatt), or "the very stamp of his nature" (RSV). "Character," originally, is the instrument used in carving or engraving. Then it is the mark (figure or letters) stamped upon the instrument itself, or stamped by it on the substance on which it is applied; then, the exact expression of any person or thing, the stamped likeness, the exact reproduction; then, by metonymy, the peculiarity by which persons or things are recognized and distinguished. The use of the word goes back to the days when every brick manufactured on the plains of Shinar or by the banks of the Nile received its graven stamp designating the ruler by whose order that brick was made.

A man's character, therefore, is the self-revelation of that by which he is ruled. In common usage it has come to stand for that which a man is, apart from and back of all opinion concerning him, or, his self-revelation as we may read it in his deeds. We are all busy each moment in this self-revelation. "We are like the weaver," one has said, "who plies his shuttle and fills in the web, thread by thread, making a pattern we do not see. We work on the wrong side, like him, and do not see what to all others is clear."

It is evident, therefore, that a man's character is independent of his reputation and circumstances. A man may be held in high repute by the world, and yet may be a despicable character. Gloucester's confession, "And seem a saint when most I play the devil," might fall from many lips. You do not know the true man until you have followed him to his home, to the secret place where he communes with his own heart. Many a saint vanishes when he enters the door of his own house. "Those uniforms," said the Duke of Wellington, "are great illusions. Strip them off, and many a pretty fellow would be a coward, when in them he passes muster with the rest."

Nor is eccentricity character. Many of us who would not judge a man by his clothes or the kind of house he lives in are misled by personal eccentricities. They do not come from nor do they indicate the inner nature. Dr. Samuel Johnson had the habit of twirling and twisting his fingers and laying his hand on every post he passed. Those were eccentricities, but his character was shown in his standing with bared head at the old bookstall in Uttoxeter market in self-imposed penance for his disobedience to his father years before.

Character is the revelation of what a man would be,

of the impulses which deliberately determine his actions, of the goals he has set before him to attain. Life at its best — so are we constituted — is a matter of imitation, or, better, of inspiration, and character is our expression of what we are making of it. If we trace back to their inception the characteristics which now mark us most distinctively, we shall find that we owe their development not so much to training as to the sudden disclosure of their attractiveness in one who had won our admiration. The personal character of a revered parent or an admired teacher has done as much to put noble ideals into many a boy's breast as the discipline of the classroom. Our ideals make us what we are. When General Grant was asked what made him a soldier, he replied, "The impressions of General Scott at West Point."

> The thing we long for, that we are
> For one transcendent moment.

It is perfectly clear, then, what makes Christian character. One word tells us. "And we all, with unveiled face beholding the glory of the Lord, are being changed into his likeness from one degree of glory to another; for this comes from the Lord who is the Spirit." We seek the highest when we look upon that Face, and every man who comes to Jesus sees the image of himself as he is in the thought of God, the man he might be, the man he ought to be; John, the "son of thunder," becomes "the beloved disciple"; Peter, the fickle, becomes "the rock." The turning-point in a man's life is how he looks upon that "glory."

O Love Who formedst me to wear
The image of Thy Godhead here;
Who soughtest me with tender care
Through all my wanderings, wild and drear;
O Love, I give myself to Thee,
Thine ever, only Thine to be.

The rock on which Jesus said He would found His Church is not Christ alone, it is not Peter alone, even taken as a type, nor is it his confession alone. It is a human person confessing Christ. It is a repenting sinner acknowledging Christ as the Son of the living God.

Abdel Ross Wentz

19
The Church

"Be good, and you will be lonely" was one of Mark Twain's aphorisms; but it is not true. There was an hour in one boy's life when he thought it was. He had just been confirmed, the only boy in a class of eleven. As he came out of the church, there were a number of his school chums, mostly of families whose churches did not have the rite of confirmation, lined up, not to congratulate him but to sneer at what they thought his weakness. They were the boys of his Zouave company and his Oliver Optic club. Never had he felt more lonely. How the first Christians must have suffered in similar loneliness, either before their Jewish companions or the Roman challenge "Diana or Christ!"

Well, he had made his choice. He would be "a lone ranger," but he would not deny Him whose thorn-crowned head in a copy of Guido Reni's great picture looked down at him from the wall of his little room. He was too young to understand that he had been initiated into the greatest fellowship the world has ever known.

The glorious company of the Apostles praise Thee;
The goodly fellowship of the Prophets praise Thee,
The noble army of Martyrs praise Thee;
The holy Church throughout the world doth acknowledge Thee.

If men were never to meet together as religious beings, it has been said, it would be as though the great reservoir which supplies a great city with water suddenly should run dry. Here and there a few might draw water from their own wells, but the general result would be appalling. The Church is a reservoir of spiritual fellowship and power. It is that because it is a divine-human institution. It is not self-originated. It grew out of multiplied experience of personal discipleship. Jesus was the founder of the Church. The Church is a fellowship of men and women, first with Jesus Christ the divine Lord and Saviour, and then, through Him, with one another. "The rock on which Jesus said He would found His Church is not Christ alone, it is not Peter alone, even taken as a type, nor is it his confession alone. It is a human person confessing Christ. It is a repenting sinner acknowledging Christ as the Son of the living God." [1] That experience, personal trust in Christ and the confession of it, and consequent fellowship with Christ, multiplied by the number of those sharing the experience, makes the Church.

It will be seen at once that the Church, by its very constitution, gathering up in itself countless confessions of faith in Jesus Christ, is a great reservoir of power, and through its ministry of Word and sacraments conveying to those confessors all that Jesus meant to His disciples when He was visibly present in the flesh — and more, as He promised — is the greatest fellowship in the world. We may not say that a man cannot be a Christian if he is not a member of the Church, but he is an abnormal Christian, as much of an alien in the Christian community as a

---

[1] Abdel Ross Wentz, *New Testament Commentary*, United Lutheran Publication House, Philadelphia.

foreigner who refuses to become naturalized in the state.

There is no fellowship comparable with the fellowship of the Christian Church. First of all, it arises from our common relationship to Jesus Christ. "I have called you friends." He said that, not to a Nicodemus coming alone by night for fear of what his fellow-Jews might say, but He said it to the Twelve as they were gathered about Him at the Last Supper, the men who had been His companions throughout His ministry and were drawn together by the magnetism of that relation. There is nothing in the whole history of the world like the bond which ties believers to Jesus Christ. He is the magnet, we are the filings. It is a fellowship without caste, or class, or preferment. The Church is the family of Jesus Christ.

The family is self-explanatory. There is no mystery or darkness in it. We do not raise questions as to the justice of a mother's love or a father's forgiveness; we do not begin to discuss rights when the stronger bear the heavier burdens and the younger learn by simple duties, each preferring the others in honor. Love is the law of the family; sympathy flows from heart to heart and passes like golden coin from hand to hand, ever reaching out, under the spell of the family tradition, even to those not thus gathered in the mystic circle, clinging closer to one another as the storms of life beat heavier and heavier. There is no question as to the meaning of such fellowship. It is the one unselfish corporation in the world, paying the highest dividends on the lowest assessments. We have said it all when we call the Church the family of Christ.

In the twilight of today I see on the horizon — not the man of Moscow, not the man of Munich, not the man of Rome, but the man of Galilee. . . . This is the message for the Church of today and for mankind milling round like sheep without a shepherd. The Man of Galilee is, and remains, our one and only Leader.

Jan Smuts

20
Our Leader

Pastor Martin Niemoeller came into disfavor with a considerable number of Americans because of his frank words: "The greatest shortcoming of the Weimar Republic was that it never could impose authority on the German people who longed for such authority." Pastor Niemoeller is a genuine German, and a man with a military record in the First World War, but he was not a Nazi. He said he had his *Fuehrer*, but it was not Hitler. "My *Fuehrer* is Jesus Christ."

When in the post-Pentecostal days, the Apostles were arrested and jailed for their activities in preaching the Gospel, and the angel of the Lord delivered them, their defense was that they had a Leader whom they must obey. The word "leader" is used four times in the New Testament. It is a military term. It means "one who takes the lead." In this respect we may compare Jesus with Joshua; the names are the same in the original tongue. Joshua was the captain of the Lord's hosts who led Israel to the Promised Land; Jesus is the captain of our salvation.

As we have said, "leader" is a military term, and in our hatred of war we are likely to forget the militant character of Jesus. We think of His meekness, His gentleness, His patience. Our favorite pictures of Him are with little children climbing upon His knees, and of His feeding the weary multitudes. But beneath the gentle and solicitous countenance of those pictures there is fire in His eyes in the presence of evil. It burned when he drove out the money changers from the temple, and to the prisoner on Patmos "His eyes were as a flame of fire . . . and He treadeth the wine press of the fierceness and wrath of Almighty God." We must not forget that Jesus was the victorious foe of the devil, and that the heroic virtues of the Conqueror were in that meek King whose weapon was love, but wielded with a soldier's hand.

Jesus has always appealed to strong men. Napoleon, Thomas Jefferson, and Jan Smuts are but a few of those who have bowed before Him. The testimony of Field Marshal Smuts has been made Tract 272 by the American Tract Society. Speaking at the centennial of the Dutch Reformed Church of Potchefstroom, in the Transvaal, in February, 1942, the field marshal said: "Speaking from longer and wider experience and reflection than perhaps has been the lot of most others, I wish to say: fundamentally the world has no need of a new order or a new plan, but only of the honest and courageous application of the historical Christian idea. Our Christian civilization is based on eternal order, an endless plan in the message of Christ. Many new messages and messengers will appear in these times of great tribulation. Let us hold on to the eternal message. Let us follow the light which once shone before us, the greatest light that has ever arisen on the human horizon, and which can surely lead us to that better world for which we are longing. In the twilight of today I see on the horizon, not the man of Moscow, not the man of Munich, not the man of Rome, but the Man of Galilee. . . . This is the message for the Church of

today and for mankind milling round like sheep without
a shepherd. The Man of Galilee is, and remains, our one
and only Leader."

Jesus rightfully is our Leader because of what He has
done. He enlisted us for God. He made at-one-ment
between God and us. He met and vanquished our deadly
Foe. He lifted from us the burden of our cares. And
now He bids us share His peace. "We see not yet all
things put under him." The great Mosque of Constan-
tinople was once a Christian church, dedicated to the
Holy Wisdom. Over its western portal may still be read,
graven on a bronze plate, the words, "Come unto me all
ye that labor and are heavy laden, and I will give you
rest." Beneath the dim inscription, in unknown tongues,
noisy crowds have surged and fought and sorrowed. No
eye has looked at it, nor any heart responded. It is but
too sad a symbol of the reception which Christ's offers
meet among men. "Men do not have peace today, because
in most of them everything is topmost that ought to be
undermost, and everything is undermost that ought to be
topmost" (Alexander MacLaren). Our world is a sad
antiphon to His pleading voice. But Christ is not dis-
couraged. He won the battle for us in darker days than
ours, and at greater cost. The mob that haled Him to
His cross shouted in the derision of triumph. They
thought that they had made an end. But Peter, facing
their trial court in defense of his boldness, declared the
paradox of the ages, "You have killed the Leader of life,
whom God hath raised from the dead." Above and be-
yond the cross "His blood-red banner streams afar." It

marks His victory over our last enemy, death. The darkness most feared of men has been pierced with light; Apollyon with his black wings has been slain. Our Leader has passed through the darkness and come back again. Across the untrodden waste of darkness there is one track — it has been made by His risen feet. If He is our Leader through death into life, then all who follow in His train shall share in His victory. His leading will not end until He has brought us where He is, our ever-living and exalted Leader.

. . . one Book wherein the spirit of man has found light and nourishment, and an interpreting response to whatever is deepest in him.

Thomas Carlyle

21
The Bible

THE Bible is the handbook of personal religion. But it is not a handbook in the sense of a digest of traffic regulations, or a "layman's lawyer," or a "home physician," or an Emily Post book of etiquette. Much less is it a religious crystal ball by which we can learn our individual spiritual fortunes or the fortunes of the world. It is the record of God's revelation of himself to men and women like ourselves in the great crises of their lives in quest of their salvation from the drag of their fallen life.

The Bible is not a single book, written at one time, in one form, by one hand. It is a library of sixty-six books, some of which are separated from others by centuries of time and all the forms of literary composition. Some of it is history, written in unknown epochs by unknown writers. Some of it is poetry, varying from penitential psalms and wise reflections on human experience to the triumphant war-song and the glowing apocalypse. Some of it is ritual, and some of it is common law. Some of it is prophecy, the impassioned denunciation of sin, personal and national, and some of it is promise, the ever-brightening hope of a great deliverance and a great Deliverer to come. That is the Old Testament library. Then, after an interspace of silence, we have the New Testament library — four Gospels (missionary tracts for evangelists), a brief church history, twenty-one letters, and an apocalypse. A heterogeneous collection, but brought together in one library because throughout "one increasing purpose runs," namely, to bring to men who knew not God the knowledge of His saving love.

The Bible is the logbook of earlier voyagers on the sea of life. It has been left us for our "comfort." "For whatsoever things were written aforetime were written for our learning (instruction), that we through patience and comfort of the scriptures might have hope" (Rom. 15:4). "Comfort" (*con-fortis*) means "coming to the aid of." The Bible is the Word of God, not because no voice but God's is heard speaking, but because the Spirit of God touched men in the experiences which are recorded, and then, through this record, touches us with the quickening power with which He inspired the first recipients. It is this power to beget again the experience which the original inspiration created which makes the Bible the Word of God for us. The letters on the printed page are lifeless without the quickening Spirit and the sensitive soul. As we read the pages of the Bible we hear God speak to us individually through conscience, collectively through history, personally in meditation, but "in these last days he has spoken to us by a Son."

That is what makes the Bible the Word of God for us. Luther discerned it and almost naively said, "Herein agree all the genuine holy books, that they all preach and exhibit Christ." By "Christ" Luther meant "salvation." What the Bible contains that gives it unity in all its parts is the message of salvation. This, said Luther, lies enshrined in all the books, and not a series of trick symbols which spell J-E-S-U-S, or any other hidden cipher by which we may have access to heaven or may spell out the future.

Christ is the Word of God. The Old Testament looks forward to Him; the New Testament bears witness to Him. The Bible is not the object of our faith; Christ is the object of our faith. The Bible is the nourisher of our faith; "that we . . . through comfort of the scriptures might have hope." The Bible keeps Christ ever before us. If He is in us and His Spirit is in us, our thoughts and our deeds will be right. "It is," says Dr. C. C. Morrison, "like a photograph of his mother which a young man takes with him into the army. He turns to it again and again to keep visibly before him the dear countenance which he cannot now see face to face." [1] The photograph is very dear to him, but it is not his mother.

The life of Jesus Christ is the incarnate Word of God. We find it easy to fall back upon the words of Christ — particularly the Sermon on the Mount — and say, "Here is the Word of God." Apart from Christ those words are our condemnation, for apart from Him not one of us can fulfill those high ideals. That is why Luther preferred the Gospel of John to the other Gospels; he was not looking for more rules of "the good life" but for power to be a better man. It is like a resurrection to get that power. "I am the vine; ye are the branches"; "I am the door of the sheep"; "I am the bread of life"; "I am the resurrection and the life" — these and words like them, whether from Jesus' lips or relayed by His missionaries, are the heart of the Word of God.

---

[1] *The Christian Century.*

The Bible, therefore, is not simply a book to analyze and classify and otherwise master as a mental task. It is a book to live with, because Christ is good to live with. If we could have Christ in the flesh, we should not need the Bible, but we need everything that helps us to have His spirit, and the Bible comes first. It was fitting that the old family Bible contained a register of the children of the family entered as they were born, baptized, confirmed, married and finally laid to rest.

"In the poorest cottage," said Thomas Carlyle, speaking of his native Scotland, "is one Book, wherein . . . the spirit of man has found light and nourishment, and an interpreting response to whatever is deepest in him." Its comfort has sustained our Western World for nearly two thousand years. In all those centuries the men and the women who have made our present heritage have made the words of that Book the songs of their pilgrimage. What histories of character, what triumphs of faith, what baptisms of hope have flowered from its precious seed! Will their children forsake it?

*Here, O my Lord, I see Thee face to
    face;*
*Here do I touch and handle things un-
    seen;*
*Here grasp with firmer hand th' eternal
    grace,*
And all my weariness upon Thee lean.

                              Horatius Bonar

22

The Sacraments

AT FIRST thought the Sacraments seem remote from personal religion. They are objective; personal religion, as we have been considering it, is mainly subjective. They confront us, in their communal setting, as the acts of the Church in which the individual is apparently passive. In the majority of the elements of personal religion enumerated in the preceding meditations the individual will was the key to its realization: In the Sacraments, while faith is the key to their realization, it does not occur to the average Christian that it is the faith of personal religion. The Church is so manifestly the agent in the ministration of the Sacraments that we have been wont to classify them entirely in the category of formal religion.

Particularly is this true of infant baptism. What participation can the infant in its mother's arms have in personal religion? That query brings us up sharply with the error in our common thinking that personal religion is wholly subjective. We miss the heart of the Christian religion if we overlook or forget the fact that God consciously and deliberately initiates the process of our religious experience and thereby reveals himself in the experience. It was to give emphasis to this truth that the liturgists of our church in Europe addressed the questions in the baptismal formula to the child: "Dost thou renounce?" "Dost thou believe?" The answer of the parents to those questions was not a make-believe substitution, but a recognition of the grace that seeks and saves even the least in the scale of the human family. In the words of an alternate formula by a beloved teacher of theology, "Baptism is not an unmeaning or empty ceremony from which the mind can receive no instruction or the heart no comfort, but it impressively brings to our remembrance that God has graciously included our children with us in His covenant of mercy toward our race." That is, it is the declaration of His grace to us singly and individually, and thereby it becomes the first element of personal religion. The failure to recognize and keep in mind the great objective reality on which our faith rests has been one of the weak points in the personal religion of professing Christians.

When we turn to the Lord's Supper there is or should be no doubt as to the place its observance holds in personal religion. "Given for you"; "shed for you." The fountain source of personal religion is the realization of the grace of God. The sacrament of the Supper brings that grace to each member of the body of Christ. The faithful use of that sacrament is the evidence of our co-operation with Christ in the building of Christlike character in us. It is like the faithful taking of the remedy our physician has prescribed for us. We may refuse it — and remain ill. We may — it is in our power — keep Christ out of our lives. That is the tragedy of our freedom.

No picture of Christ is more popularly known than Holman Hunt's "The Light of the World," the original of which hangs on the walls of Keble College, Oxford. It is a marvelous picture, of exquisite coloring and detail.

Even the facets of the jewels on the robe of Christ and the veins on the fallen leaves stand out. In the foreground is a cottage, neglected and falling to ruin. The approach is clogged with thistles, and the unmown grass and weeds tell the kind of life that is lived there. In front of the fast-closed door a tall and stately figure stands amid the night dews and the darkness, with a face that tells of long and weary waiting. His right hand is knocking at the door, while his left hand holds a lantern, by the light of which the face is seen, a crown of thorns upon His head. The words that come to our lips at once as we look at the picture are, "Behold, I stand at the door and knock."

Two things are suggested for personal religion by the picture. The first is that Christ is the aggressor and comes knocking at our door. The second needs an additional word concerning the picture. When the canvas was finished, we are told, Holman Hunt invited a friend to come and inspect it, and after looking at it steadily for a few minutes he said, "Holman, the picture is beautiful, but you have made a strange omission in it. You have painted a door without a latch. Who ever heard of a door without a latch?" "You have missed the point of the picture," exclaimed the artist. "There is no latch to that door. If there were, do you think the Saviour would be standing outside for admission?"

"What makes me a man," says George Matheson, "is just my power to open the door. . . . Jesus would have no joy in coming in if I did not open the door."

The symbolic significance of the sacraments is just that: we open the door, we think to make Jesus our guest, and lo! He becomes the host. There is a little poem that has gone the rounds of devotional reading and perhaps has been forgotten. It describes the desolate soul sitting alone with Sorrow. "Lamp and fire were out; the rain wildly beat upon the window pane." There was a knock at the door, and a hand upon the latch. Could it be that there was a visitor in such a night? But a reassuring voice replied, "I am come to sup with thee."

> All my room was dark and damp;
> "Sorrow," said I, "trim the lamp;
> Light the fire and cheer thy face;
> Set the guest-chair in its place."
> And again I heard the knock;
> In the dark I found the lock;
> "Enter; I have turned the key —
>   Enter, Stranger!
> Who art come to sup with me."
>
> Opening wide the door He came,
> But I could not speak His name;
> In the guest-chair took His place;
> But I could not see His face!
> When my cheerful fire was beaming,
> When my little lamp was gleaming,
> And the feast was spread for three,
>   Lo! my Master
> Was the guest that supped with me.

That may be poor theology, but it is good religion. In life's dark hours we need the objective reality which the sacrament gives. Chaplains of World War II tell us that in their ministrations to the dying their most common request was for the sacrament. The battle had been a great objective reality — their souls cried out for something to match it. In the sacrament they saw their Lord and heard His Voice, as in the battle they had given the last full measure of their devotion to their line commander. Mere words seem too poor in such an hour.

I fear no foe, with Thee at hand to bless
Ills have no weight, and tears no bitterness.
Where is death's sting? Where, grave, thy victory?
I triumph still, if Thou abide with me.

Hold Thou Thy cross before my closing eyes,
Shine through the gloom and point me to the skies;
Heaven's morning breaks, and earth's vain shadows flee;
In life, in death, O Lord, abide with me.

Jesus Christ was an event in and through which "the living God" Himself is offered for our apprehension.

John Knox

23

"What Think Ye of Christ?"

THE passing of Mr. H. G. Wells in the year of our Lord 1946 removed not only one of the most colorful figures in the literary world of our generation but also one of the most brilliant and provocative of contemporary critics. He was a historian, a novelist, and an economic prophet — more successful in the first and second roles than in the last; he predicted that he would live to be 97, but he died at 79.

In his *Outline of History* he must needs deal with Jesus. His picture of Jesus is as fanciful as some of his imaginary excursions. He does not admit the New Testament writers as competent witnesses. Of necessity he must accept their testimony of fact, for we have no other source from which to draw a portrait at all. He ignores them, however, whenever their testimony conflicts with his axioms of history. Jesus was a great teacher who taught a revolutionary doctrine of the Fatherhood of God, which, were it accepted, would mean a world revolution. He was a man of brilliant genius and exalted character, but, stripped of the fanciful interpretation of His followers, He was only a revolutionary, "a lean and strenuous person," who was put to death for His teaching. True, He insisted that the kingdom of God which He proclaimed was not of this world, but the common people understood Him literally and tried to make Him a king. This frightened the authorities, and they crucified

Him. Then the rumor went about that He was alive; His disciples believed the rumor and created the Christian Church. So much, says Mr. Wells, is history.

Is that all? It is also history that revolutions perish when their promoters are put out of the way. They have their day and cease to be. But here is a man who was ignominiously put to death and yet today is the most powerful influence in the world. The signs of His supremacy are everywhere. The stream of His influence has been enriching the centuries. The sound of His voice has never died away. He is a living presence. The ideals He embodied have been the guiding star of our best endeavor. Instinct, habit, custom, and law in our life at its best have been penetrated and transformed by His presence. The whole sweep of our civilization has been played upon, awakened, and wrought over, so that, in spite of brutal resistance and cruel persecutions, He emerges the undying One in the cataclysms of the centuries. We could more easily pluck the sun out of the sky than think Him out of our life. Our whole thought of God and man, our entire working philosophy of life, is everywhere encompassed and interpenetrated by Christ.

> Through Him the first fond prayers are said
> Our lips of childhood frame;
> The last low whispers of the dead
> Are burdened with His name.

When we ask ourselves how this has come about, we are driven back to the source-books of the New Testament, and the earliest of these are the letters of Paul. These

letters have little to say about the life and deeds of Jesus,
but they are flooded with Christ. Their entire uplook
into heaven and their outlook upon the world are but
different phases of the dominating soul of the Master.
He lives in Paul, and Paul lives in Him. He has led that
proud Pharisee captive and made him His bond-servant.
There was no room for the self-deception of fanaticism.
The best-trained mind among the Apostles had to surrender to the overwhelming evidence of Christ's appearance to him. It was the evidence which the writers of the
Gospels later collated. The man Jesus was something
more than a starry-eyed revolutionist. His self-styled
mission was not to drive the Romans out of Palestine and
restore a purified Jewish state. His interest was not in
metes and boundaries, wages and possessions. His interest
was the eternal righteousness of God. His ethic was uni-
versal, not an "interim" ethic. As Prof. John Knox has
said, "Jesus as an ethical teacher belongs to all the generations just because he did not, in a sense, belong to his
own." [1] He announced His mission in the words, "The
Son of man is come to seek and to save that which is
lost." He would find in every man what He found in
Zacchaeus — what everybody else had failed to see — a
soul; others saw only a purse. He found a soul also in the
intruder in the house of Simon the Pharisee. The woman
saw something more in Him than "a lean and strenuous"
revolutionary. One cannot read the Gospels as they have
come down to us without being impressed by the fact that

---

[1] *Christ the Lord*, Willett, Clark & Co., Chicago.

Jesus' primary interest was the righteousness of God in the souls of men. He is the physician of the soul, not merely, like John the Baptist, the herald of a physician. It is not good history not to take that into account. Jesus taught that if the individual soul was brought into right relation with God all human relations in life would fall into line. He refused to become the umpire of property inheritance (Luke 12:13, 14); He refused to lead a Zionist uprising (Luke 19:41-44); His one concern was that men should know God as He knew Him. He came preaching the Good News of the kingdom: "God so loved the world that he gave his only Son, that whosoever believeth in him should not perish but have everlasting life" (John 3:16). He touched earth's unfortunates with healing power. He called the Twelve to be the agents of this ministry. He went to publicans and sinners because "the whole need not a physician, but they that are sick" (Matt. 9:12). He declared Himself to be "the light of the world" (John 8:12); in wisdom, "a greater than Solomon (Matt. 12:42); in time, "before Abraham was" (John 8:58). He commanded His people to honor Him as they honored God the Father (John 8:54); He revised the law of Moses on His own authority (Matt. 5:21, 22); He prescribed prayer to the Father in His name (John 15:16); He raised the impotent and forgave his sins (Mark 2:5); He cast demons from tortured souls (Matt. 8:16; Luke 8:2); He raised the dead (Mark 5:41; Luke 7:11ff.); He foretold His own death and resurrection and steadfastly set His face to go up to Jerusalem where His prediction was fulfilled (Matt. 16:21ff.); He told Pilate that He was a king,

but not of this world (John 18:37); He forgave the
penitent thief on the cross and promised him an entrance
into His kingdom (Luke 23:39-43); He rose from the
dead and commissioned His disciples to remit and retain
sins (John 20:23) and to proclaim His gospel throughout
the world (Matt. 28:19ff.).

What think ye of Christ? It is His question. The
Roman soldier at the cross said, "Truly he was Son of
God." He was an unconscious prophet of Christendom.
That confession, without word or document of authenti-
cation, epitomizes the faith of the Apostolic Church. As
Prof. John Knox puts it, "Jesus Christ was an event in
and through which 'the living God' Himself is offered
for our apprehension." [2] But the question has a reverse
as well as an obverse, and it too must be faced. What does
Christ think of me? And that will be the final question.
Have it out now, friend. He is the standard by which
all men are going to be judged. Richard Watson Gilder
fell on his knees before that standard and made his great
confession. Is it yours?

> If Jesus Christ is a man
> And only a man, I say
> That of all mankind I will cleave to Him
> And to Him will I cleave alway.
>
> If Jesus Christ is a God
> And the only God, I swear
> I will follow Him through heaven and hell,
> The earth, the sea, and the air.

[2] *Ibid.*

I am the resurrection and the life. He that believeth in me, though he were dead, yet shall he live. And whosoever liveth and believeth in me shall never die.

John 11:25-26

24
Eternal Life

AND THEN? No other generation in history has witnessed such a holocaust of life as ours. Not since the days of Ashurnasirpal has the world witnessed such ruthless slaughter. The mortality of World War II made it a nightmare of madness. Human life sank to a new low in the scale of values. It is not strange that a new pessimism has fallen upon the young survivors of the war. Our chaplains tell us that their young men, many of them at least, have become our modern Sadducees with regard to eternal life.

Human life has always been cheap. The mortality of war has not been as great as that of the years of peace. In her long history England put more men to death for petty crimes than she lost on the battlefield. Seventy-two thousand heads are said to have fallen in the reign of Henry VIII, and capital punishment for theft continued until the beginning of the past century. Can we believe in eternal life and snuff out human life like a candle?

But that in reality is not the question. Can we rid ourselves of "the intimations of immortality," however we humiliate human life? The future life is not so much a fact that can be demonstrated as a corollary of our consciousness. "Man has everywhere interpreted his destiny as higher than that of the grass that withers and the beasts that perish." Belief that there is a future life is not a matter of logic but of instinct. It is an old principle of mental science that every instinct has its correlate to match it. The air matches the wing of the bird; the water, the fin of the fish; light, the eye; sound, the ear; beauty, the sense of beauty; the relation of cause and effect, the reasoning faculty; the future life, the soul that cries out for it. We know that the mind is manifested by its own consciousness; that intelligence is not a matter of chemical reactions or glandular activity; that decay of the physical organism does not involve the apprehensive faculty. Animals are not mocked by their instincts, nor man by his intuitions. There is in every human soul a void that nothing earthly or transitory can fill. "If I am wrong," said Cicero, "in believing that the souls of men are immortal, I please myself in my mistake. . . ." In a poem which he never gave to the public, Bayard Taylor has given wings to the urge which every thoughtful soul since the days of Job has felt:

> . . . Proven by its needs:
> By fates so large no fortune can fulfill,
> By wrongs no earthly justice can atone,
> By promises of love that keep love pure,
> And all rich instincts powerless of aim,
> Save chance, and time and aspiration wed
> To freer forces, follow. By the trust
> Of the chilled Good that at life's very end
> Puts forth a root, and feels its bosom sure!
>
> .   .   .   .

The climax of the book of Job is reached in the *impasse* of issues which our present experiences do not solve, when the God who manifests himself on earth is against him, while the God whose face is for the moment hid from him is for him. "Even now, when all seems lost, when he all but feels the icy hand of death upon his body, he has his Witness in heaven, and knows that he shall stand before Him." "This body may break up, but even then my life shall have a vision of God" (Moffatt).

"Do you think," said Socrates to his disciples as he was about to drink the hemlock, "that I am a less skillful diviner than the swans which sing longest and sweetest in the prospect of death?" But that did not satisfy Simmias. He could not trust the unknown so placidly. He wanted to know what was in store for him on the other side of death. He felt that he must deal with such a problem more heroically, guided only by our present experience and the laws and limitations of our present existence. "We must gain one of two results: either man must discover the whole truth about the fundamental meaning of life, here and hereafter, or, if that be impossible (and all human striving shows that it is), we must take the best and truest of human words, and, supported on this as on a raft, sail through the waters of life in perpetual jeopardy, unless we might make the journey on a securer stay — some divine word, it might be — more surely and with less peril." [1]

How human the wish of Simmias! All serious men have cherished it. Without the word of prophecy made more sure, the darkness is as dense for us as it was for

---

[1] F. J. Church, *The Trial and Death of Socrates* (Phaedo), The Macmillan Company, New York, 1903.

him. The great, deep sea of mystery that immerses us is uncharted and unplumbed. No one has of himself reached the first result proposed by Simmias, has of himself got a clear insight into the meaning of life, here and hereafter. The most inspiring of human words have indeed been as rafts on which we "sail through the waters of life in perpetual jeopardy."

But we have "the word of prophecy more sure" — the risen Lord and His benediction of peace. "And when he had so said, he showed unto them his hands and his side. Then were the disciples glad when they saw the Lord." It was that vision that changed the faces of believers as they faced the future. "I am the resurrection and the life. He that believeth in me, though he were dead, yet shall he live. And whosoever liveth and believeth in me shall never die." This is the "someone" for whom Simmias yearned. He is here. It is enough.